Welcome to London!

I have been living in London since 2016. My husband's job transferred him here, and we were newly empty nesters with the last of our two sons off to university. So we thought, why not? Why not sell the house in Pasadena, get rid of most of our possessions, and pack up and move to London? We had been once before and loved it. We are native Californians, but both of us have lived various places. I'd lived in Berkeley, San Francisco, NYC (including Brooklyn), and Los Angeles. I knew I was a city girl who loved the stimulation and excitement of the big city. Pasadena was a smaller, more suburban city, and we stayed there because we were raising my children and our families lived in the area. But once we were done raising children, we were looking for our next adventure, and the offer to move to London came at the perfect time.

I had been working in real estate before we moved to London, working on a family team at Sotheby's International in Pasadena, helmed by my mother who had more than 30 years' experience. She brought me and my sister into the fold, but my background before that was in publishing and freelance writing, where I was a food writer.

When we first arrived, we were shown flats by a relocation company paid by my husband's job. We stayed in corporate housing for 30 days whilst I did the flat search while he worked. I think I naively assumed that things worked the same way they did back in the States (both on the tenant side and also as an agent) ...boy was I wrong. But I've learned a lot over the years. I've personally dealt with relocation companies as a client, I've been a tenant, I've purchased property, and I'm also a real estate agent, which they call an estate agent here.

I've had to learn some new terminologies and very different systems of renting and buying property. I've seen so many questions in the online ex-pat groups, and I've answered a lot of them as well. I created this e-book with the idea that this is something I wish I'd had when I first came to London. This e-book deals strictly with the processes of renting and purchasing property, not on matters regarding attaining a visa to come to the UK or other immigration issues. But if you have questions regarding UK visas, the UK government's "How to Apply for a Visa To Come to the UK" is a good place to start.

I hope that you find the information in this guide helpful.

Lonnée Hamilton
Director, London Realty International
WhatsApp: +44 7535 604 111
Email: hello@londonrealtyinternational.com
www.londonrealtyinternational.com

KEY QUESTIONS
to help you get started

- ✓ What type of apartment are you looking for? Are you sharing with a roommate? What style is best for you? Period? New build?

- ✓ What kind of neighbourhood appeals to you?

- ✓ How many bedrooms and bathrooms do you need?

- ✓ What are you looking for in a kitchen?

- ✓ What is your preferred layout?

- ✓ What is your budget?

- ✓ Are you looking for furnished or unfurnished

- ✓ What about storage space? Closets? Basements, lockers?

- ✓ Do you need a garage or extra parking spaces?

- ✓ Do you have a pet?

- ✓ How is your daily commute? How easy is it to get to the places you need to go?

- ✓ How close do you need to be to transit, shopping, schools, hospitals?

RENTING IN LONDON

TABLE OF CONTENTS

- **01** TOP TIPS FOR MOVING TO LONDON
- **02** THE LINGO
- **03** CHOOSING A NEIGHBOURHOOD
- **04** US vs UK ESTATE AGENCY
- **05** RENTING IN LONDON: WINNING THE GAME
- **06** PROPERTY LETTING GLOSSARY
- **07** HOW TO RENT GUIDE & SAMPLE AST TENANCY AGREEMENT
- **08** LETTING CHEAT SHEET

1 TOP TIPS FOR MOVING TO LONDON

London is undoubtedly one of the best cities in the world. Its diverse culture, great career opportunities, and general high quality of life are all key features that make it an attractive destination for expats from across the globe. If you truly wish to unlock the full potential of London life, though, you must put the right preparations in place.

Here are some things you should do for the smoothest possible move. Doing these in advance helped me with my move from Los Angeles to London. I hope that they help you as well.

RENTING IN LONDON

PREPARE FOR LIFE IN A SMALLER PROPERTY

London is one of the best cities in the world, but it's also one of the most expensive. The harsh reality, then, is that it's likely you will need to downsize your property. Rather than transporting unneeded assets to London, use this as an opportunity to declutter and earn a little extra cash. You can further support your preparations for life in London by going paperless and considering furniture with hidden storage – like ottomans and similar pieces.

TV wall brackets and shelving can be used once you move in to aid the cause even more. Facebook groups like Expat Swap Meet are good sources for pre-owned furniture. David Phillips offers full furniture packages both for purchase and rental of new furniture.

FIND THE RIGHT PART OF LONDON FOR YOU

London is home to 14 million people. Naturally, then the contrast of housing prices across different parts of the city is huge. As well as financial fluctuations, you'll want to think about schooling, transports facilities, crime rates, and other factors that could influence your daily life in a big way. Moreover, you may want to look for an area with amenities that appeal to your background – whether it be cultural or recreational passions or hobby preferences.

If you are trying to narrow down an area based on travel commute, I recommend Zoopla's Commuting Times Calculator. You aren't only investing into a home; you're starting a new life. Make it count.

OPEN A UK BANK ACCOUNT

Opening a UK bank account can be a little tricky if you try whilst you are still overseas. Most UK banks require two forms of identification, one being a UK proof of address. Broadly speaking, these include:

- a tenancy agreement or mortgage statement;
- a recent electricity or gas bill (less than 3 months old);
- a recent (less than 3 months old) bank or credit card statement that's not printed off the internet; or
- a current council tax bill.

If you haven't moved yet, or are still in transition with your housing situation, then your proof of address isn't readily available and you may have to wait until you are settled in order to open the account.

Alternatively, you could open a Wise.com borderless multi currency account, which allows you to pay and get paid in multiple currencies. You can convert your money between the supported currencies for a small fee and transfer the money to a local bank account. You will also be able to get a debit card connected to your borderless account, which will make it even easier to pay for your life in the UK.

Your home bank may be able to set up an account for you if it has a correspondent banking relationship with a British bank. Many major UK banks also have so-called 'international' accounts. These are designed specifically for non-residents, so they're a great option if you don't have the documents to prove your UK address. In fact, you can even apply for an international account online. Barclays, Lloyds, HSBC and NatWest all offer international bank accounts.

Some find online-only banks like Starling or Monzo an easier option than traditional banks.

GET CONNECTED

Facebook groups for expats like Americans in the UK, American Expats of Colour in the UK, Americans in London, and Americans in the United Kingdom, a Helpful Expat Group can help answer many of your initial questions and are a great resource for asking questions about your move.

Once you arrive in London, there are numerous social clubs for ex-pats like The American Women's Club in London, various university alumni networks, and The University Alumni Club of London. African American sororities AKA and the Deltas have London offshoots.

Private clubs have a long and storied history in London and many people join private clubs like The Arts Club or Soho House. Women's private clubs like The Allbright and The Wing can be useful in making social and business connections. Private clubs have a membership approval process and be prepared to pay as they are not inexpensive.

2 THE LINGO

A lot of people make the mistake in thinking that just because the U.S. and the U.K. are both English speaking countries, that the terminology is going to be the same. Generally speaking, it is. But there are some crucial differences in the property business that might trip you up if you don't know them ahead of time.

RENTING IN LONDON

London is divided into *boroughs*, which are like counties but still part of Greater London. There are 32 London borough councils, and each council v its own *council tax*, which is paid monthly. Tenants are responsible for paying council tax (not landlords). Full-time students are exempt from paying council tax. Homeowners are responsible for paying council tax. When you move into a new property, you should immediately register with the council as the council tax payee. Council tax varies regarding the assessed value of the property and is grouped by bands.

Estate agent is what we call a real estate agent in the States. Realtor is not a term used in the UK. An agent who specialises in letting is a *letting agent*.

Flat is an apartment. The term apartment is also used, but generally I've seen apartment used in luxury buildings. Flat is the more commonly used term.

High street is what we could call the main street of a neighbourhood. It's where the majority of the shops and restaurants are located. Most London neighbourhoods have a high street.

Letting is the same as renting. Both terms are used but letting is more traditional. An apartment that has been rented has been *let*.

There are two primary portals used for property searches: *Rightmove* and *Zoopla*. These are the equivalent to Zillow in the States and what you will use for looking for property.

Postcodes are the equivalent to Zip Codes. Postcodes in London are quite useful for gauging what area a property is in. Generally speaking, the first part of the postcodes are the same as compass points: N = north; W= west; S = south; E= east; SW = southwest, etc.

These directionals tell you what part of London the property is located. After the compass point comes a number. 1 means that the location is closest to the center, with numbers getting higher the farther out you go. So a property in N1 is in north London but closest to the center. When people say South London, they are generally speaking about London south of the river, but there are postcodes such as SW in Chelsea and Fulham are north of the river.

Property is the term more commonly used than real estate. I've been seeing some estate agents use "real estate" lately (maybe because of the American real estate shows), but property is the term that most people use.

A *TV licence* is required if you play any programme on a TV or computer or mobile phone if you watch live TV, or if you download BBC iplayer. You can be fined if you watch TV without a licence.

VAT is sales tax and is charged for most goods or services.

3 PARTS OF LONDON

This is just a rough overall bird's eye view of what neighbourhoods are located where. I didn't include every part of London. But this is just to give you a larger sense. People all the time ask me what areas they should live in, but London neighbourhoods are so diverse, and it really depends on what you are looking for.

RENTING IN LONDON

NORTH LONDON

Neighbourhoods include areas such as: Angel, Hampstead, Highgate, Belsize Park, St. John's Wood, Primrose Hill, West Hampstead, Golders Green, Crouch End and Hampstead Garden Suburb.

Vibe: Green, leafy, hills, parks, lots of American ex-pats (Hampstead, St. John's Wood). Commuter friendly to The City (Angel)

EAST LONDON

Neighbourhoods include areas such as: Shoreditch, Hoxton, De Beauvoir, Dalston, Spitalfields, London Fields, Columbia Road, Bow, Hackney Wick, Wapping, Stoke Newington, Bethnal Green, Canary Wharf and Hackney.

Vibe: Hip, trendy, urban, fun, cool, coffeehouses, Regent's Canal, Williamsburg, modern (Canary Wharf).

RENTING IN LONDON

WEST LONDON

Neighbourhoods include areas such as: Marylebone, Belgravia, Fitzrovia, South Kensington, Kensington, Chelsea, Notting Hill, Holland Park, Pimlico, Earl's Court, Shepherd's Bush, Maida Vale, Paddington. Richmond and Chiswick are farther out but still part of London.

Vibe: Classic London, posh, architecture, traditional, historic, the London you see in the movies, international. Calm outside the city (Richmond and Chiswick), commuter-friendly (Paddington).

SOUTH LONDON

Neighbourhoods include areas such as: Greenwich, Brixton, Clapham, Vauxhall, Wimbledon, Peckham, Nine Elms, Battersea, and Bermondsey.

Vibe: South of the river, modern high rises (Battersea and Vauxhall), truly varied in neighbourhoods and prices, family friendly (Wimbledon and Clapham)

RENTING IN LONDON

THE CITY OF LONDON

The City is the financial district in the centre of London (think like the Downtown area of an American city). There are increasing numbers of new build residential developments located in The City. It's the oldest part of London. This is a different area than Canary Wharf, which is another financial district in East London on the River Thames.

If you are a fan of Brutalist architecture, you might want to live in The Barbican, built in the 1960s, it was one of the first mixed-used developments in the world. The concrete style isn't for everyone, but I lived there for a couple of years and really enjoyed it. The Barbican complex itself has restaurants, cinemas, theatre and art galleries.

KING'S CROSS

This is a newly regenerated area of London with a very stylish shopping and dining area called Coal Drop's Yard. There are high-rise luxury housing developments. This area has its own new postcode N1C. It's super convenient for transportation, being next to Saint Pancras and King's Cross tube station. There is an American-size Waitrose for grocery shopping.

RENTING IN LONDON

4 US VS. UK ESTATE AGENCY

This is the chapter I wish I had when I was first looking at properties when I arrived in London. It's the part that is the most different from what we are accustomed to in the US and the assumptions that the systems are the same will lead you down some convoluted paths that will leave you scratching your head wondering why you can't get what you asked for.

RENTING IN LONDON

In the US, when you want to purchase or even rent a property, you might just ask around for a good agent or find one yourself... and then you expect this person will do the legwork of making calls, setting up viewings, filtering out the places that are absolute crap. This form of estate agency DOES NOT EXIST IN THE UK in the same way. I've learned this the hard way, both as an agent and as a tenant.

In the U.S. the real estate agent is not paid by the buyer or tenant, as they are paid from the seller or landlord's side of the commission. One reason this works this way is that there is a database called the MLS (multiple listing service), where agents can go and look for properties and see what they are going to get paid. It's all upfront. For sales, commissions in the U.S. are typically paid 6%, with 3% going to the buyer's agent and 3% for the selling agent. Leases are less money but still the agent is usually paid by the landlord. (The system is a bit different in NYC). But basically, you as a buyer can pick up the phone, arrange a day of viewings with the agent and to have an agent representing you doesn't cost anything for you out of pocket.

The UK does not have an MLS. So, what this means is that the properties you find on Rightmove or Zoopla are represented by the agents listing them. Let me make this clear... the agents with properties on Rightmove or Zoopla are not your agent. They are the landlord's agent or the seller's agent and their job is to market the property and bring buyers or tenants to the property. Their contract is not with you. They have a contract with the property owner.

To make it very clear, you as the buyer or tenant do not have an agent in the transaction. You are unrepresented. Also, agents are not motivated to show you other agents' properties as commissions are much lower in the UK 1% to 2%, so agents typically aren't happy to split their commission with a buying or letting agent. Also FYI... most agents aren't even paid commission. They are employees of the agency they work for.

The majority of property transactions occur in this way. Think of it as a pair of shoes... the agent has these shoes on the shelf and that's all they're going to show you. What was confusing to me when I arrived was that I would walk into an agency thinking that the agent would find me what I want, when the reality was the agent would show me what they had on the shelf, if that make any sense. Also, because the agent has you in their database, you get inundated with other properties they are trying to sell that don't fit your criteria. You asked for a 2-bedroom with hardwood floors. If they have you in their grasp on a day of viewings, they might to try to steer you to a 1-bedroom with carpet if they don't have any more 2-bedrooms with hardwood floors. Now not every agent is this craven, but the quality varies a lot.

There are laws in place such as truth in advertising, so you are not unprotected. Also, I would say that the majority of agents want transactions to move smoothly and want happy people on both sides of the deal. But there are some dodgy ones out there.

However, in the UK there are some buyers and tenants who see the value of hiring their own agent. I think particularly if you are new to the UK and don't want to get caught up in some obvious traps, it can be worth the money to have your own agent. If nothing else they act as a buffer between you and the vendor's agent. If you are interested, you can take a look at my fees below.

Property to Rent: I charge an upfront non-refundable retainer fee upon signing of agreement of £500 including VAT. This fee is deducted from the final Success Fee.

Success Fee: 4 weeks of rent including VAT.

A bit of self-promotion is in order. I have represented buyers and sellers. I have found my buyers off-market properties just because I had good rapport with the selling agent, who told me when a deal was coming up. Also, I spend a lot of time narrowing down and previewing properties for my clients so that they don't waste time.

I had a young American couple from the Bay Area who had their heart broken trying to find their own flat for rent. They even paid a holding deposit, only to find out that the flat was rented to someone else. They didn't realise that the property was on the market with multiple competing agents and in that scenario, whomever has a tenant who signs the lease first is the one who gets the apartment. They did get their deposit back, and I helped them find a place they loved but also helped them to avoid some of the classic traps that await the unaware or newly arrived.

5 RENTING IN LONDON: WINNING THE GAME

Let's get down to brass tacks. The majority of Americans moving to London usually start out as renters when they first arrive, even if they decide to buy at a later date. People like to get a sense of the area, whether they like their neighbourhood and all that.

So here are the steps you will need to take in order to let your first London flat.

RENTING IN LONDON

RIGHTMOVE AND ZOOPLA

If you aren't hiring an estate agent then you will need to invest some time searching for properties on the portals and schedule time to go to viewings. You might need to adjust your expectations, as London is a very competitive rental market, and you might not see the amount of care and upkeep you would be accustomed to in the US. Of course this isn't the majority, but bear in mind that landlords are basically in the driver's seat and while it's good to have high standards, you might have to relax them a bit in order to be chosen as the tenant. If you find a place you absolutely love, congratulations but take a temperature read. Ask the agent if there have been a lot of viewings of the property. You can see on the portals how long it has been on the market. Most competitively priced flats are rented within a few days of being launched. It can very much be a game of early bird gets the worm, so check the portals daily and be proactive.

Sometimes agents can take a while to respond. It's not always their fault, as they are oftentimes outside the office conducting viewings. Many respond at the end of the day when they are at their desk. It pays to be a bit persistent (whilst always being polite) and I usually call/WhatsApp and email in order to get hold of the agent to schedule the viewing.

NEIGHBOURHOOD

Before you start looking at flats, take some time to go to various neighbourhoods. Walk around. Check out the high street. Does it have the neighborhood amenities you are looking for? Grocery stores, cinemas, gym? Walk down some of the residential streets and see if this is the kind of place you want to call home.

RENT CALCULATIONS

Rents in the UK are often posted as weekly rates. This can be confusing to some US renters because we assume that there are 4 weeks in a month when we calculate a weekly rent. £500/week = £2,000/month. But no... that's incorrect. Weekly rent is calculated by the number of weeks in the year. So £500/week x 52 weeks in a year = £26,000 a year. Divide the yearly amount by 12 months £26,000/12 = £2,166.66 per month.

Similarly, if the property is marketed at a monthly rate of £2,000 per month, the weekly rate would be calculated at £2,000 x 12 month = £24,000 per year. Divide that by 52 weeks and the weekly rent is £461.54.

BUDGET

One popular rule for referencing is that you need to earn 2.5 times what you spend on rent. So if you earn £2,500 per month before taxes, you should spend about £1,000 per month on rent. Sometimes a landlord will pay utilities, but usually that's not the case. Utilities include electricity, Internet, and water. It's not uncommon for tenants to offer 3 or 6 months of rent in advance, but it's not necessary to do so to let a flat.

Other costs before you move in before you move in will include:

- Your deposit, including both a holding deposit (up to 1 week's rent) and your standard security deposit (up to five weeks' rent if total annual rent is less than £50,000).
- Any removal fees such as hiring a van or a removal service
- Your first month's rent

But I'm getting a bit ahead of myself. Let's go back to the viewing.

FURNISHED VS. UNFURNISHED

You've found your perfect London flat, but it's furnished, and you hate the furniture. You want the landlord to take it all away and you want to furnish it yourself. Don't be surprised if that is a deal breaker, or the landlord comes back with a counter offer whereby you pay for transport and storage of their furniture and must replace it to where it was. It's my experience that landlords might agree to take away small pieces but are often reluctant to move beds, sofas because they don't have anywhere to keep it. Sometimes it may seem ridiculous because the sofa does not look like it's worth the storage fees, but some landlords can be a bit stubborn. Either put up with it and put a throw over the sofa, or pay for storage, or find an unfurnished flat if you feel that strongly about decor.

TOUCH-UPS

When you are at the viewing, take note of any cosmetic changes you might want because the time to ask for those are when the tenancy agreement is being drafted. I would test the waters with the agent showing the property to see what they think might be reasonable. The landlord might not agree to your accent wall, but might agree for you to do it, if it's painted back to the same colour before you move out. But I would wait until my offer is accepted before I got too much into special requests. It is a negotiation with the landlord.

OFFER ACCEPTED

Congrats! The landlord loved you and thought you will make an amazing tenant. What's next? Usually at that point you pay one week's holding deposit (see Rent Calculations) and that takes the property off the market. Double check the portals to make sure the letting agent has taken it down.

At that point most landlords and letting agents send your details to a 3rd party referencing company. This part feels very intrusive to Americans. But you must provide all the information the referencing company requires and do so in a timely manner.

REFERENCING

Referencing in the UK is thorough. The referencing company will call your employer for proof of employment and might also ask for recent pay slips and bank statements. Previous and current landlords are usually called. If there are any issues with the referencing company speaking to them or if there are other issues that might raise a red flag, it's best to be upfront with the landlord so that it does not appear that you are hiding something. If you fail referencing because of a lie you have told, then the landlord is able to keep the holding deposit as payment against wasting their time. After referencing is complete, the decision to move ahead is that of the landlord, not the letting agent.

STUDENTS

Students in the UK often pay 6 months in advance and are often asked to have a Guarantor who will be responsible for paying the rent if the student cannot. Students need to provide proof of enrollment at university they are attending. Students do not need to pay council tax. Some landlords will only accept UK guarantors. If that is a problem, there are 3rd party private guarantors like Housing Hand or Rent Guarantor that you can use. Students should request individual rather than joint tenancies, so that one student or one guarantor isn't responsible for everyone's rent.

RIGHT TO RENT

Letting agents and landlords have to be sure that anyone letting a flat in the UK has the right to be in the country and need to conduct a Right to Rent check which means that they will need to see originals of your passport and biometric residence card. If you are in the UK on a 6-month tourist visa, then you cannot rent an apartment for longer than you have the right to stay in the UK, meaning you won't be able to sign a year-long lease. I have had one client who signed a 6-month lease, but most landlords won't want to deal with that if they can get a longer-term tenant. If that is your situation, I think it's better for you to try to negotiate terms with a landlord on short term rental platforms like Airbnb or Plum Guide, which has a strict vetting process for homes.

PASSED REFERENCING!

You've made all the right moves and have passed referencing. Hurrah! Here's where you need to pony up the cash. The landlord/letting agent will register the 5 weeks deposit. So you will need to pay an additional 4 weeks because you've already paid one week as a holding deposit. You will receive a certificate with a code number that you can enter to double check that your deposit is registered.

This is where the terms of the tenancy agreement come into play. If you are asking for a break clause, minor repairs or touch-up cosmetic work ask for it now. The landlord knows that they have a good tenant, so this is really the only point where you have leverage. But be reasonable. There's no point going through all of this and unleashing an avalanche of demands that put the tenancy in jeopardy. Because until the lease is signed there is no deal and both parties can walk away.

THE LEASE

As mentioned previously, most residential tenancy agreements in London are ASTs (Assured Shorthold Tenancy). Flats rented by a business would be under a Common Lease, not an AST.

THE LEASE (CONT'D)

Gov.Uk defines the necessary parts of a tenancy agreement as follows:

A tenancy agreement should include:
• the names of all people involved
• the rental price and how it's paid
• information on how and when the rent will be reviewed
• the deposit amount and how it will be protected
• details of when the deposit can be fully or partly withheld (for example to repair damage you've caused)
• the property address
• the start and end date of the tenancy
• any tenant or landlord obligations
• an outline of bills you're responsible for

It can also include information on:
• whether the tenancy can be ended early and how this can be done
• who's responsible for minor repairs (other than those that the landlord is legally responsible for)
• whether the property can be let to someone else (sublet) or have lodgers

BREAK CLAUSE

A break clause is a clause in a fixed-term Tenancy Agreement that allows the lease to be ended early. There is no standard format for a break clause. Break clauses are not mandatory. Usually, both tenant and landlord can exercise the break clause. A typical break clause would allow either party to end the lease with two months' notice after the first 6 months. Meaning, if the tenant or landlord wished to end the least at the beginning of the break clause (month 6), then notice would need to be given in writing at month 4 of the lease. Break clauses can give tenants an out to a longer-term lease, however it can work both ways depending on the wording of the clause, with the landlord giving notice to the tenant as well.

6 PROPERTY LETTING GLOSSARY

Important letting terminology so that you understand what is being discussed and what is at stake in your property letting experience.

RENTING IN LONDON

Assured Shorthold Tenancy (AST) is the most common form of lease/tenancy agreement for letting a residential property with rents up to £100,000 per year. If your rent is more than £100,000 per year, you would sign a Common Lease, but the vast majority of residential leases will be ASTs. Citizen's Advice provides guidance as to what a tenancy agreement should contain.

Break clause lays out the ways in which a lease may be "broken" before the end of the fixed term. The wording of the break clause should be carefully gone over. Shelter goes into much more detail about the various kinds of break clauses. Just know that the lease is a legal document and whatever you sign in the lease will be hard to change at a later date.

Fixed term tenancy agreement is a lease that lasts for a set amount of time, usually six months to a year. Unless there is a break clause, the tenant is responsible for all of the rent in the fixed term. After a fixed term tenancy agreement ends, it may be renewed as another fixed term tenancy agreement. Unless the tenant gives notice, a fixed-term tenancies converts to a periodic tenancy, or what we would call month-to-month in the States.

Gas Safety Certificate should be provided by the landlord or letting agent if you have any gas appliances in the property upon signing of your tenancy agreement.

Guarantor is someone who agrees to be responsible for the payment of your rent should you not be able to pay it. A guarantor is usually a family member or close friend. They should have a good credit rating. Some landlords require guarantors to be UK based and property owners.

HMOs (Houses of Multiple Occupancy) are properties where three or more unrelated people share a common area like a bathroom or kitchen. HMOs must be licensed.

How To Rent Guide is provided by the UK government. It has been provided in Chapter 7. You should receive one from the landlord or letting agent upon signing of your tenancy agreement.

Inventory is a check-in report about the physical state of the property. Tenants can pay to have a professional inventory done, or do their own inventory by taking photos. Landlords may also have their own inventory done. Regulations in the UK tend to favour landlords, so it's in your best interest to have as complete an inventory done as possible.

Periodic tenancy is what we would call a month-to-month agreement in the States. All fixed term tenancies automatically become periodic tenancies unless the tenant gives written notice to the landlord.

Tenancy deposit scheme or deposit protection scheme. Unlike in the US, the word "scheme" in the UK doesn't have nefarious connotations of something shady. It just means a plan or policy in government or business. Tenancy deposits are held by a third party that protects your funds from being stolen. After you sign the tenancy agreement and pay the full security deposit, the landlord or letting agent must register your deposit in the scheme and provide you with a certificate.

Since 2019, *tenant fees* are illegal. Letting agents and landlords are not allowed to require tenants to pay for things like inventory or agency fees. More information about the Tenant Fees Act is available at https://www.gov.uk/government/publications/tenant-fees-act-2019-guidance

8 LETTING CHEAT SHEET

I know... so. many. words. And you are a busy person. Here's what you need to know about renting a property in a nutshell. I do think though, that you might find the long version helpful. But these are the Cliff's.

RENTING IN LONDON

LETTING CHEAT SHEET

01 Search for properties on the portals (Rightmove, Zoopla).

02 Attend viewings

03 Make offer / Offer accepted.

04 Pay holding deposit (one week's rent to be applied to security deposit)

05 Go through referencing (provide all requested documentation quickly).

If you are using a Guarantor they will usually be required to go through some form of referencing. Requirements will change whether the Guarantor is in the UK or outside the country..

RENTING IN LONDON

LETTING CHEAT SHEET

06 Sign tenancy agreement. Along with the lease signed by both parties, your landlord must also have given you a copy of the leaflet 'How to rent: the checklist for renting in England', an energy performance certificate, and a gas safety certificate if there are any gas appliances.

07 Pay security deposit – 5 weeks for rent under £50k per year; 6 weeks rent for over £50K per year. Pay one month's rent (or more if part of tenancy agreement).

08 Receive security deposit registration certificate

09 Conduct your own inventory or agree to landlord's inventory if amenable.

10 Move in.

RENTING IN LONDON

9 HOW TO RENT GUIDE & SAMPLE AST

LONDON REALTY INTERNATIONAL

RENTING IN LONDON

HOW TO RENT GUIDE

RENTING IN LONDON

HOW TO...
RENT

The checklist for renting in England

Part of the How to Guides series

HM Government

HOW TO RENT   2

Contents

1. Assured shorthold tenancies 3	**5. Living in your rented home** 11
2. Before you start 4	The tenant must… 11
Key questions 4	The tenant should… 11
Ways to rent a property 5	The landlord must… 12
	The landlord should… 12
3. Looking for your new home 6	**6. At the end of the fixed period** 13
Things to check 6	If you want to stay 13
Licensing requirements 8	If you or the landlord want to end the tenancy 13
4. When you've found a place 9	**7. If things go wrong** 15
Check the paperwork 9	Protection from eviction 16
	8. Further sources of information 17

Please be aware that some advice in this guide may be affected by the latest coronavirus (COVID-19) guidance for renting.

Please refer to guidance for landlords, tenants and local authorities reflecting the current COVID-19 outbreak.

The landlord, or the letting agent, should give the current version of this guide to the tenant when a new assured shorthold tenancy starts. There is no requirement for a landlord to provide the document again if the assured shorthold tenancy is renewed, unless the document has been updated.

Who is this guide for?

This guide is for people who are renting a home privately under an assured shorthold tenancy, either direct from a landlord or through a letting agency. Most of it will equally apply if you are in a shared property but in certain cases, your rights and responsibilities will vary.

The guide does not cover lodgers (people who live with their landlord) or people with licences (such as many property guardians – see this specific guidance) – nor tenants where the property is not their main or only home.

December 2020

1. Assured shorthold tenancies

When you enter an assured shorthold tenancy – the most common type – you are entering into a contractual arrangement.

This gives you some important rights as well as some responsibilities.

This guide will help you to understand what your rights are, what responsibilities you have and what questions to ask.

This will help you create a positive relationship with your landlord, but will also tell you how to get help if things go wrong.

Take your time to read documents and contracts carefully. When you rent a home, people sometimes expect you to make a quick decision, or to sign documents before you've had time to think about them.

You shouldn't feel forced into a decision and it is important to understand the terms and conditions of any contract you are agreeing to before you sign it.

Your landlord must provide you with a copy of this guide, so **use the checklist and keep it safe** to protect yourself from problems at every stage.

2. Before you start

Key questions

- **Is the landlord or letting agent trying to charge any fees?** For example, for holding the property, viewing the property or setting up a tenancy agreement? Since 1 June 2019, most fees charged in connection with a tenancy are banned. A charge to reserve a property is permitted but it must be refundable and it cannot equate to more than 1 weeks' rent. Viewing fees and tenancy set-up fees are not allowed. See 'Permitted fees' below for more details.

- **How much is the deposit?** Since 1 June 2019, there has also been a cap on the deposit that the tenant is required to pay at the start of the tenancy. If the total annual rent is less than £50,000, the maximum deposit is 5 weeks' rent. If the annual rent is £50,000 or above, the maximum deposit is 6 weeks' rent. The deposit must be refundable at the end of the tenancy, usually subject to the rent being paid and the property being returned in good condition, and it must be 'protected' during the tenancy. See 'Deposit protection' below.

- **How long do you want the tenancy for?** The landlord must allow you to stay in the property for a minimum of 6 months. Most landlords offer tenancies for a fixed term of 6 or 12 months. However, it is possible to negotiate a longer tenancy. Alternatively, you could agree to a tenancy which rolls over on a weekly or monthly basis. These tenancies have no fixed end date, but the landlord must allow you to stay in the property for at least 6 months.

- **What can you afford?** Think about how much rent you can afford to pay: 35% of your take-home pay is the most that many people can afford, but this depends on what your other outgoings are (for example, whether you have children).

- **Are you are entitled to Housing Benefit or Universal Credit?** If so, you may get help with all or part of your rent. If you are renting from a private landlord you may receive up to the Local Housing Allowance (LHA) rate to cover or help with the cost of rent. Check with this online calculator to see if you can afford to live in the area you want. You should also look at this advice about managing rent payments on Universal Credit.

- **Which area you would like to live in and how you are going to look for a rented home?** The larger the area where you are prepared to look, the better the chance of finding the right home for you.

- **Do you have your documents ready?** Landlords and agents will want to confirm your identity, immigration status, credit history and possibly employment status.

- **Do you have the right to rent property?** Landlords in England must check that all people aged 18 or over, living in their property as their only or main home have the right to rent. Landlords must carry out this check before the start date of your tenancy agreement. There are two types of right to rent checks; a manual document-based check or a check via the Home Office online checking service. Your landlord can't insist which option you choose but not everyone can use the online service.

    Further information on how to prove your right to rent to a landlord can be found on GOV.UK.

- **Will you need a rent guarantor?** Some landlords might ask someone to guarantee your rent. If you don't have a guarantor, you can ask Shelter for advice.

HOW TO RENT 5

Ways to rent a property

Direct from the landlord

- ☐ Look for landlords who belong to an accreditation scheme. Accreditation schemes provide training and support to landlords in fulfilling their legal and ethical responsibilities. Your local authority can advise you about accreditation schemes operating in your area. The National Residential Landlords Association and the Guild of Residential Landlords run national schemes.

Through a letting agent

- ☐ Letting agents must be a member of a redress scheme. You should check which independent redress scheme the agent is a member of in case you have an unresolved dispute.

- ☐ If they receive money from you such as rent payments, you should also check they are a member of a client money protection scheme. See a list of approved schemes. By law, this information should also be clearly visible to you at the agent's premises and on their website.

- ☐ Reputable agents are often accredited through a professional body such as ARLA Propertymark, GPP , Safeagent, RICS or UKALA.

Watch out for scams!
Be clear who you are handing money over to, and why.

3. Looking for your new home

Things to check

- ☐ **Deposit cap.** Check that the tenancy deposit you're being asked for is not more than 5 weeks' worth of rent (where annual rent is less than £50,000) or 6 weeks' rent (where annual rent is more than £50,000).

- ☐ **Deposit protection.** If the landlord asks for a deposit, check that it will be protected in a government approved scheme. Some schemes hold the money, and some insure it. You may be able to access a bond or guarantee scheme that will help you put the deposit together. Contact your local authority for advice.

- ☐ **You may be offered a deposit replacement product as an alternative to a cash deposit.** A landlord or agent cannot require you to use a deposit replacement product but may allow it as an option without breaking the Tenant Fees Act. There are several different deposit replacement products available on the market. Depending on the product, you may be required to pay a non-refundable fee up-front (often equivalent to one week's rent) and/or a monthly payment for the duration of your tenancy. With most products you will still be responsible for the costs of any damages incurred at the end of the tenancy or required to pay an excess on any claim for damages or unpaid rent. It is strongly advised to always check the terms and conditions and to see if it is regulated by the Financial Conduct Authority (FCA).

- ☐ **Length of tenancy.** There is usually a fixed period of 6 or 12 months. If you want more security, it may be worth asking whether the landlord is willing to agree to a longer fixed period. Alternatively, you may be offered a weekly or monthly assured shorthold tenancy which does not last for a fixed period. Even with those tenancies, however, the landlord must allow you to stay in the property for a minimum of 6 months.

- ☐ **Smoking and pets.** Check if there are any rules about them, as well as for other things such as keeping a bike, dealing with refuse and recycling.

- ☐ **Bills.** Check who is responsible for bills such as electricity, gas, water and council tax. You or the landlord? Usually the tenant pays for these. Advice on paying bills is available here.

- ☐ **Fixtures and fittings.** Check you are happy with them, as it is unlikely that you will be able to get them changed once you have moved in.

- ☐ Smoke alarms **and** carbon monoxide detectors. Landlords must have **at least** one smoke alarm installed on every storey of a property they let out. In addition, if you have solid fuel appliances like wood burning stoves or open fires, check carbon monoxide detectors must be provided. If not, your landlord must install them. They could save your life.

- ☐ **Safety.** Check that the property is safe to live in. Use the How to rent a safe home guide to help you identify possible hazards.

- ☐ **Fitness for human habitation.** Your property must be safe, healthy and free from things that could cause serious harm. If not, you can take your landlord to court. For more information, see the tenants' guide on using the Homes (Fitness for Human Habitation) Act 2018. You should also check whether your tenancy agreement excuses you from paying rent should the building become unfit to live in because of, for example, a fire or flood.

Check who your landlord is

Make sure you have the name of your landlord and an address in England or Wales where the landlord will accept service of notices, in writing. Landlords are obliged to provide you with this information and the rent is not 'lawfully due' until they do so.

If the property is a flat, ask whether the landlord is the owner or leaseholder of the flat, and ask whether the freeholder, for example the owner of the block, has agreed to the flat being let out. If the landlord has a mortgage ask whether the mortgage company has agreed to the letting. The landlord may not need the freeholder's consent but, if there is a mortgage, the lender's consent will always be needed. Be aware that you may have to leave the property if the landlord does not keep up the mortgage payments.

If the property is a house, ask whether the landlord is the owner, whether the landlord has a mortgage and whether the mortgage company has agreed to the letting. You may have to leave the property if the landlord does not keep up the mortgage payments.

If the 'landlord' is not the property owner – and they claim to be a tenant, a family member or a friend, be very cautious, as it could be an unlawful sub-letting.

Permitted fees

The government's guidance on the Tenant Fees Act contains information about the fees that letting agents and landlords are prohibited to charge tenants, as well as the fees that are permitted.

Permitted fees are as follows:

- [ ] rent
- [ ] a refundable tenancy deposit capped at no more than 5 weeks' rent where the total annual rent is less than £50,000, or 6 weeks' rent where the total annual rent is £50,000 or above
- [ ] a refundable holding deposit (to reserve a property) capped at no more than 1 week's rent
- [ ] payments associated with early termination of the tenancy, when requested by the tenant
- [ ] payments capped at £50 (or reasonably incurred costs, if higher) for the variation, assignment or novation of a tenancy
- [ ] payments in respect of utilities, communication services, TV licence and Council Tax
- [ ] a default fee for late payment of rent and replacement of a lost key/security device giving access to the housing, where required under a tenancy agreement

All other fees, including the following, are banned:

- [ ] viewing fees, any charge for viewing the property
- [ ] tenancy set up fees, any charge for setting up the tenancy or contracts
- [ ] check out fees, any charge for leaving the property
- [ ] third party fees, any charge for anything that is done by someone other than the landlord or tenant but that the landlord must pay for

Licensing requirements

Houses in Multiple Occupation (HMOs)

HMOs are usually properties where three or more unrelated people share facilities such as a kitchen or bathroom.

Some HMOs must be licensed. Check that your landlord has the correct licence. Landlords of licensed HMOs **must by law** give tenants a statement of the terms on which they live in the property.

Selective Licensing

Some single family dwellings may also need to be licensed. Check with your local authority whether the house is within a selective licensing scheme area. Selective licensing enables a local housing authority to require all landlords of privately rented housing in a designated area to obtain a licence for each individual property. It gives the local housing authority powers to inspect properties and enforce standards to address specific property issues.

4. When you've found a place

Check the paperwork

- ☐ **Tenancy Agreement.** Make sure you have a written tenancy agreement and read it carefully to understand your rights and responsibilities before you sign it. The landlord or agent usually provides one, but you can ask the landlord or agent to consider using a different version instead. The government has published a model tenancy agreement which can be downloaded for free. If you have any concerns about the agreement, seek advice before you sign. If you are unhappy with the tenancy agreement, the Tenant Fees Act allows tenants to walk away from unfair terms without forfeiting the holding deposit.

- ☐ **Inventory.** Agree an inventory (or check-in report) with your landlord before you move in and, as an extra safeguard, make sure that you take photos. This will make things easier if there is a dispute about the deposit at the end of the tenancy. If you are happy with the inventory, sign it and keep a copy. From 1 June 2019, landlords/letting agents cannot charge certain fees – see the government's guidance for more information.

- ☐ **Meter readings.** Remember to take meter readings when you move in. Take a photo showing the meter reading and the date and time, if possible. This will help make sure you don't pay for the previous tenant's bills.

- ☐ **Contact details.** Make sure that you have the correct contact details for the landlord or agent, including a telephone number you can use in case of an emergency. You are legally entitled to know the name and address of your landlord.

- ☐ **Code of practice.** Ask whether your landlord or agent has signed a code of practice, which may give you additional assurance about their conduct and practices.

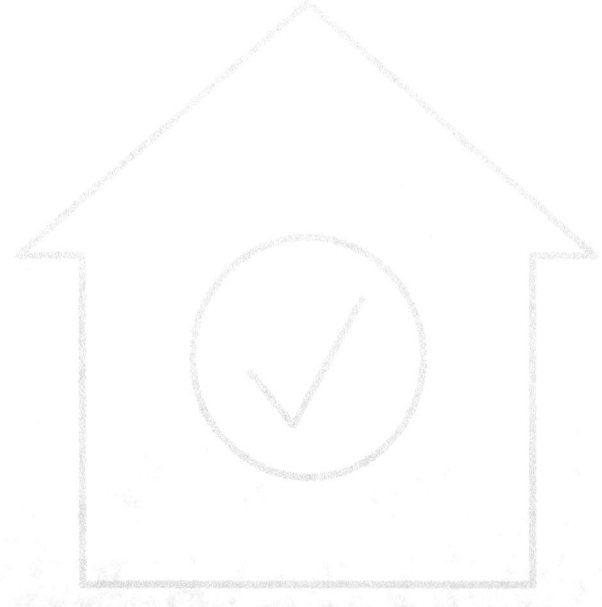

The landlord must provide you with:

- [ ] A copy of this guide 'How to rent: the checklist for renting in England' when a new tenancy starts as a printed copy or, if you agree, via email as a PDF attachment.

- [ ] A gas safety certificate. The landlord must provide you with a copy of this certificate before you enter into occupation of the property and must give you a copy of the new certificate after each annual gas safety check, if there is a gas installation or appliance.

- [ ] Deposit paperwork. If you have provided a deposit, the landlord must protect it in a government approved scheme within 30 days and provide you prescribed information about it. Make sure you get the official information from your landlord, and that you understand how to get your money back at the end of the tenancy. Keep this information safe as you will need it later.

- [ ] The Energy Performance Certificate (EPC). Your landlord must provide you with a copy of the EPC, which contains the energy performance rating of the property you are renting, free of charge at the onset of your tenancy. As of April 2020, all privately rented properties must have an energy performance rating of EPC Band E or above (unless a valid exemption applies) prior to being let out. You can also search online for the EPC and check its rating on https://www.epcregister.com/.

The landlord should also provide you with:

- [ ] A record of any electrical inspections.

- [ ] Under the Electrical Safety Standards in the Private Rented Sector (England) Regulations 2020, landlords have to get their property electrics checked at least every five years by a properly qualified person. This applies to new tenancies from 1 July 2020 and existing tenancies from 1 April 2021. The electrics must be safe and your landlord must give you proof of this. For more information please see our guidance on electrical safety standards in the private rented sector.

- [ ] Evidence that smoke alarms and any carbon monoxide alarms are in working order at the start of the tenancy. Tenants should then regularly check they are working.

5. Living in your rented home

The tenant must...

- **Pay the rent on time.** If your rent is more than 14 days late, you could be liable for a default fee. A default fee for late payment of rent is limited by the Tenant Fees Act to interest on the outstanding amount, capped at 3% above Bank of England base rates. The landlord/agent cannot charge any other fees. For more information, please read the Government's guidance for tenants on the Tenant Fees Act 2019. Further, you could lose your home because you have breached your tenancy agreement. If you have problems, GOV.UK has links to further advice. Check out these practical steps for paying your rent on time.

- **Pay any other bills** that you are responsible for on time, such as council tax, gas, electricity and water bills. If you pay the gas or electricity bills, you can choose your own energy supplier.

- **Look after the property.** Get your landlord's permission before attempting repairs or decorating. It's worth getting contents insurance to cover your possessions too, because the landlord's insurance won't cover your things.

- **Be considerate to the neighbours.** Anti-social behaviour may be a reason for your landlord to evict you.

- **Not take in a lodger** or sub-let without checking whether you need permission from your landlord.

The tenant should...

- Make sure you know how to operate the boiler and other appliances and know where the stopcock, fuse box and any meters are located.

- Regularly test your smoke alarms and carbon monoxide detectors – at least once a month.

- Report any need for repairs to your landlord. If you think there are any repairs that are needed, you should report these to your landlord. Failure to report the need for repairs could be a breach of your tenancy agreement. In extreme circumstances there may be a risk to your deposit if a minor repair turns into a major problem because you did not report it.

- Consider obtaining insurance for your contents and belongings – the landlord will usually have insurance for the property but it will not cover anything that belongs to you.

- Consider if having a smart meter installed would save you money, if you are responsible for paying the energy bills. Read guidance about your rights and information about how to get a smart meter. We'd recommend that you tell your landlord before you get one.

- And don't forget to register to vote.

HOW TO RENT 12

The landlord must…

- [ ] **Maintain the structure** and exterior of the property.

- [ ] **Ensure the property is free from serious hazards** from the start of and throughout your tenancy.

- [ ] **Fit** smoke alarms on every floor and carbon monoxide alarms in rooms with appliances using solid fuels – such as coal and wood – and make sure they are working at the start of your tenancy. If they are not there, ask your landlord to install them.

- [ ] **Deal with any problems** with the water, electricity and gas supply.

- [ ] **Maintain** any appliances and furniture they have supplied.

- [ ] **Carry out most** repairs. If something is not working, report it to your landlord or agent as soon as you can.

- [ ] **Arrange an annual** gas safety check by a Gas Safe engineer (where there are any gas appliances).

- [ ] **Arrange a five-yearly electrical safety check** by a qualified and competent person (this applies to new tenancies from 1 July 2020 and existing tenancies from 1 April 2021).

- [ ] **Seek your permission to access your home and give at least 24 hours' notice of proposed visits** for things like repairs and those visits should take place at reasonable times – neither the landlord nor the letting agent is entitled to enter your home without your express permission.

- [ ] **Get a licence for the property** if it is a licensable property.

- [ ] **Ensure the property** is at a minimum of EPC energy efficiency band E (unless a valid exemption applies).

The landlord should…

- [ ] Insure the building to cover the costs of any damage from flood or fire.

- [ ] Check regularly to ensure all that products, fixtures and fittings provided are safe and that there haven't been any product recalls. Help is available at the Royal Society for the Prevention of Accidents (ROSPA), Trading Standards and the Child Accident Prevention Trust.

- [ ] Ensure blinds are safe by design and they do not have looped cords. This is especially important in a child's bedroom. More information can be found at https://www.rospa.com/campaigns-fundraising/current/blind-cord.

6. At the end of the fixed period

If you want to stay

Should you wish to extend your tenancy after any initial fixed period, there are a number of important issues to consider. Check Shelter's website for advice.

Do you want to sign up to a new fixed term?

If not, you will be on a 'rolling periodic tenancy'. This means you carry on as before but with no fixed term – your tenancy agreement should say how much notice you must give the landlord if you want to leave the property – one month's notice is typical. Shelter publishes advice on how you can end your tenancy.

Your landlord might want to increase your rent

Your landlord can increase your rent by agreement, or as set out in your tenancy agreement, or by following a procedure set out in law.

> The deposit cap introduced by the Tenant Fees Act 2019 means you may be entitled to a partial refund of your tenancy deposit. The government's guidance on the Act explains whether this affects you.

If you or the landlord want to end the tenancy

> The government has announced that it plans to put an end to 'no fault' section 21 evictions by changing existing legislation. Landlords will still be able to issue you with a section 21 possession notice until new legislation comes into effect. If you receive a section 21 notice from your landlord, seek advice from Shelter or Citizens Advice. If you are eligible for legal aid, you can also contact Civil Legal Advice for free and confidential advice.

There are things that both landlords and tenants must do at the end of the tenancy:

Giving notice

It is a legal requirement for landlords to give you proper notice if they want you to leave, and they can only legally remove you from your home with a court order. Normally, the landlord must allow any fixed period of the tenancy to have expired, and they must have given you the correct period of notice, which varies depending on the type of tenancy and the reason your landlord wants you to leave.

If you have been served with a notice that your landlord wants you to leave, you should read it at once. The notice should contain helpful information. Acting on it straight away may, in certain circumstances, allow you to keep your home. If you are unsure how to respond or worried that you will become homeless, you should access advice and support as soon as possible, for example through contacting Citizens Advice and/or Shelter, who can provide free, expert advice on your individual circumstances. If you are eligible for legal aid, you can also contact Civil Legal Advice for free and confidential advice.

For more information about your rights and responsibilities when your landlord wants you to leave your home, see Understanding the possession action process: A guide for private landlords in England and Wales.

If you want to end the tenancy

Your tenancy agreement should say how much notice you must give the landlord if you want to leave the property. One month's notice is typical. If you want to leave the property, you must give notice to your landlord in writing – make sure you keep a copy of the document and a record of when it was sent. Please see 'If things go wrong' below if you wish to leave sooner than the notice period set out in the tenancy agreement.

Rent

Make sure that your rent payments are up to date. Do not keep back rent because you think that it will be taken out of the deposit.

Bills

Do not leave bills unpaid. This might have an impact on your references and credit rating.

Clear up

Remove all your possessions, clean the house, dispose of rubbish and take meter readings. Try to leave the property in the same condition that you found it in. Check this against your copy of the inventory and take photos that show how you have left the property.

Dispose of any unwanted furniture via a local collection service.

Return the keys

Return all sets of keys that were provided. If you do not, the landlord may charge you for changing the locks.

Inspection

Try to be present when the property is inspected to check whether any of the tenancy deposit should be deducted to cover damage. If you do not agree with proposed deductions contact the relevant deposit protection scheme.

7. If things go wrong

Most problems can be resolved quickly and easily by talking to your landlord or letting agent.

There are often legal protections in place too for the most common problems that you may experience during the tenancy – the following links will tell you what they are or where to look for help:

- ☐ **If you have a complaint about a letting agent's service** and they don't resolve your complaint, you can complain to an independent redress scheme. Letting agents must be a member of a government approved redress scheme.

- ☐ **If you wish to leave the property within the fixed term, or more quickly than permitted in the tenancy agreement** you should discuss this with your landlord. If your landlord or letting agent agrees to end the tenancy early, you should make sure that this is clearly set out in writing and that you return all your sets of keys. If you do not, your landlord may make a court claim against you, to obtain possession of the property. You could be charged if you want to end the tenancy early, although this fee must not exceed the loss incurred by the landlord or the reasonable costs to your letting agent if you are renting through them. Unless or until a suitable replacement tenant is found, you will be liable for rent until your fixed-term agreement has ended or, in the case of a statutory periodic tenancy, until the required notice period under your tenancy agreement has expired. The government's guidance on the Tenant Fees Act contains more information.

- ☐ **If you are having financial problems**, or are falling into rent arrears, speak to your landlord as they may be helpful, and are likely to be more sympathetic if you talk to them about any difficulties early on. Should you need further help contact your local housing authority, Citizens Advice or Shelter as soon as possible. If you are eligible for legal aid, you can also contact Civil Legal Advice for free and confidential advice. Check out these practical steps for managing your rent payments.

- ☐ **If the property is in an unsafe condition** and your landlord won't repair it – contact your local authority. They have powers to make landlords deal with serious health and safety hazards. You can also report this to your local Trading Standards.

- ☐ **You may be able to take your landlord to court yourself** if you think the property is not fit for habitation, under the Homes (Fitness for Human Habitation) Act 2018. The court can make the landlord carry out repairs and can also make the landlord pay you compensation. You may also be able to take your landlord to court if they do not carry out some repairs. For more information, please see the Shelter advice on section 11 of the Landlord and Tenant Act 1985.

- ☐ **If you have a serious complaint about the property** and your local authority has sent a notice to the landlord telling them to make repairs, your landlord may not be able to evict you with a section 21 notice (no fault eviction) for 6 months after the council's notice. You can still be evicted with a section 8 notice if you break the terms of your tenancy.

- ☐ **Failure to comply with a statutory notice is an offence.** Depending on the notice, local authorities may prosecute or fine the landlord up to £30,000. **Local authorities have powers to apply for** banning orders which prevent landlords or property agents from managing and/or letting out property if they are convicted of certain offences. If a landlord or property agent receives a banning order, they will be added to the Database of Rogue Landlords and Property Agents. There is a specific process for this, which can be found here.

- ☐ **If a landlord or letting agent charges you a prohibited payment** (a banned fee according to the Tenant Fees Act 2019) or unlawfully retains a holding deposit they could be liable for a fine of up to £5,000 and if there are multiple breaches they could be liable for a fine up to £30,000 as an alternative to prosecution. Local authorities are responsible for issuing these fines. Landlords or letting agents cannot rely on giving notice under section 21 to obtain a possession order if they have not repaid any unlawful fees or deposits they have charged under the terms of the Act.

- ☐ **If your landlord is making unannounced visits or harassing you** – contact your local authority, or if more urgent dial 999.

- ☐ **If you are being** forced out illegally contact your local authority. Shelter and Civil Legal Advice (see Help and Advice below) may also be able to help you. If your landlord wants you to leave the property, they must notify you in writing, with the right amount of notice. You can only be legally removed from the property if your landlord has a court order for possession and a warrant is executed by court bailiffs or sheriffs.

- ☐ If you live with your partner and you separate, you may have the right to carry on living in your home.

- ☐ **If you are concerned about finding another place to live**, then contact the Housing Department of your local authority straight away. Depending on your circumstances, they may have a legal duty to help you find accommodation and they can also provide advice. The local authority should not wait until you are evicted before taking action to help you.

If you are concerned about finding another place to live, then contact the Housing Department of your local authority straight away.

Protection from eviction

Landlords must follow strict procedures if they want you to leave your home. They may be guilty of harassing or illegally evicting you if they do not follow the correct procedures.

Landlords must provide you with the correct notice period and they can only legally remove you from your home by obtaining a court order for possession and arranging for a warrant to be executed by court bailiffs or sheriffs. See Understanding the possession action process: A guide for private residential tenants in England and Wales.

Rent Repayment Orders

Rent Repayment Orders require a landlord to repay a specified amount of rent to a tenant and/or a local authority, where there has been, for example, an illegal eviction or failure to licence a property that requires licensing.

Rent Repayment Orders also cover breach of a banning order or failure to comply with certain statutory notices. Where a Rent Repayment Order is made, local authorities may retain the money if the tenant's rent was paid by state benefits. Where a tenant has paid rent themselves, the money is returned to them. If benefits covered part of the rent, the amount is paid back pro-rata to the local authority and the tenant.

If you are reading a print version of this guide and need more information on the links, please contact us or on 0303 444 0000 or at 2 Marsham Street, London, SW1P 4DF.

8. Further sources of information

Read further information about landlords' and tenants' rights and responsibilities.

Read the government's guidance on the Tenant Fees Act. This includes:

- **what the Tenant Fees Act covers**
- **when it applies and how it will affect you**
- **helpful Q&A**

Tenancy deposit protection schemes

Your landlord must protect your deposit with a government-approved tenancy deposit scheme.

- Deposit Protection Service
- MyDeposits
- Tenancy Deposit Scheme

Client money protection schemes

Your agent must protect money such as rent payments through membership of a government approved client money protection scheme.

Letting agent redress schemes

Every letting agent must belong to a government approved redress scheme.

- The Property Ombudsman
- Property Redress Scheme

Homes (Fitness for Human Habitation) Act 2018

Guide for tenants

Help and advice

- Citizens Advice – free, independent, confidential and impartial advice to everyone on their rights and responsibilities.
- Shelter – housing and homelessness charity who offer advice and support.
- Crisis – advice and support for people who are homeless or facing homelessness.
- Your Local Housing Authority – to make a complaint about your landlord or agent, or about the condition of your property.
- Civil Legal Advice – if you are eligible for legal aid, you can access free and confidential advice.
- Money Advice Service – free and impartial money advice.
- The Law Society – to find a lawyer.
- Gas Safe Register – for help and advice on gas safety issues.
- Electrical Safety First – for help and advice on electrical safety issues.
- Marks Out Of Tenancy – information for current and prospective tenants.

Also in this series

The government's How to rent a safe home guide helps current and prospective tenants ensure that a rented property is safe to live in.

The government's How to let guide provides information for landlords and property agents about their rights and responsibilities when letting out property.

The government's How to lease guide helps current and prospective leaseholders understand their rights and responsibilities.

The government's How to buy a home guide provides information to home buyers.

The government's How to sell a home guide provides information to those looking to sell their home.

SAMPLE AST TENANCY AGREEMENT

RENTING IN LONDON

The Parties to this agreement and the Premises

The following clauses set out the basic terms of the tenancy, the main dates and the Deposit and Rent amounts which have been agreed. Below are defined terms which will have the meaning listed next to them in this agreement.

This agreement is made the day of 01 January 2021.

Premises	123 Sample Road London A1 1AA together with fixtures, furniture and effects therein as specified in the inventory
Landlord	Landlord Notices should be sent to 124 Sample Road London A1 1AA
Tenant	[Awaiting Name Confirmation] Notices should be sent to 123 Sample Road London A1 1AA
Guarantor	[Awaiting Name Confirmation]
Occupancy	The maximum number of people permitted to occupy the property is 2
Term	A fixed term of 12 months Commencing on and including 01 January 2021 To and including 31 December 2021 ("the Initial Term") And then continuing as a monthly contractual periodic tenancy until terminated in accordance with this agreement
Rent	£1,000.00, one thousand GBP per month, payable in advance on or before the 1st day of each month (a "Rent Payment Day")
Deposit	£1,000.00, one thousand GBP

1. The Landlord lets to the Tenant the Premises for the Term at the Rent specified above.

2. The Tenant shall pay to London Realty International on the signing of this agreement the amount of the Deposit and the first payment of Rent, unless the Tenant and the Landlord have agreed in writing a later date when payment may be made. This agreement shall not become binding on the Landlord until the Tenant has paid the Deposit and the first payment of Rent, and the Tenant shall have no right to occupy the Premises, until this payment has been made in full.

3. The Deposit will be paid to London Realty International and held under the terms of mydeposits, of which London Realty International is a registered member. Further detail is provided in the next section of this document.

4. The first payment of Rent will be paid to London Realty International and held by London Realty International up to a maximum of 14 days from

the beginning of the Term, after which it will be paid to the Landlord with London Realty International's fees deducted where applicable.

5. The Tenant shall pay all future Rent when it becomes due, either to London Realty International, or the Landlord directly; the Tenant will be notified in writing of the correct account details for payment. Further detail is provided in subsequent sections of this document and in London Realty International's Terms of Business.

6. It is a condition of this agreement that the Tenant and any occupiers of the Premises over the age of 18, at all times maintain a right to rent in accordance with and as defined by the Immigration Act 2014 (where applicable). If the Tenant does not provide satisfactory documentation to allow the Landlord to verify the Tenant's identity and to satisfactorily perform any right to rent immigration checks required, the Landlord will not permit the Tenant to occupy the Premises.

7. This agreement is intended to create an Assured Shorthold Tenancy as defined by section 19A of the Housing Act 1988 (as amended).

The Deposit

The following clauses set out:

- what London Realty International will do with the Deposit paid by the Tenant under clause 3 above;
- what the Tenant can expect of the Landlord or London Realty International when either deals with
- the Deposit;
  the circumstances in which the Tenant is entitled to less than the full Deposit returned at the
- conclusion of the tenancy; and
  the circumstances in which other monies may be requested from the Tenant.

By signing, all parties declare that the details relating to the Deposit that are outlined in this tenancy agreement are correct to the best of their knowledge and belief.

8.1. The Deposit will be held in a Custodial Tenancy Deposit Scheme by mydeposits, which is the Government approved custodial scheme:

mydeposits
1st Floor Premiere House
Elstree Way
Borehamwood
Hertfordshire
WD6 1JH

Phone: 0333 321 9401

Fax No: 0845 634 3403

Email: businessdevelopment@mydeposits.co.uk

More information can be found in the deposit scheme guide and on the mydeposits website.

8.2. Once the Deposit has been paid by the Tenant, London Realty International will promptly transfer the Deposit to mydeposits. London Realty International will aim to do this within 1 working day of funds clearing, and always within the 30 days required under the terms of the scheme. Once funds have cleared with mydeposits, the Deposit will be re-assigned to the Landlord's registered account with mydeposits.

8.3. The Tenant is not entitled to receive any interest on the Deposit. At the end of the tenancy, howsoever it comes to an end, upon vacant possession of the Premises and return of the keys, the Deposit shall be returned to the Tenant less such sum as the Landlord may reasonably require:

- to pay any arrears of Rent;
- to make good any damage to the Premises and fixtures and fittings (except for fair wear and tear) caused by the Tenant or arising from any breach of the terms of this agreement by the Tenant or the Tenant's failure to take reasonable care;
- to make good any damage caused or cleaning required due to pets, animals, reptiles, birds, or fish occupying the Premises (whether or not the Landlord consented to its presence);
- to pay any sum repayable by the Landlord to the local authority where housing benefit has been paid direct to the Landlord by the local authority;
- to compensate the Landlord for any other breach by the Tenant of the terms of this agreement;
- to pay any unpaid account or charge for water, electricity, gas, other fuels or utilities used by the Tenant in the Premises;
- to pay any unpaid council tax, telephone charges or other monies owed by the Tenant to the Landlord;
- to compensate the Landlord for any reasonable cost incurred to clean the Premises to the same standard as at the beginning of the tenancy;
- to compensate the Landlord for the charges incurred by the Landlord's bank if any cheques or standing orders from the Tenant are not honoured by the Tenant's bank.

8.4. No deductions shall be made from the Deposit unless, or until, the reason for the nature of the deductions along with their amounts have been notified to the Tenant. Any dispute arising from the proposed deductions will be subject to mydeposits guidelines including use of the free and independent Alternative Dispute Resolution service where its use has been agreed by the Tenant and Landlord.

8.5. The Tenant shall not be entitled to withhold the payment of any instalment of Rent or any other monies payable under this agreement on the ground that the Landlord, or London Realty International, holds the Deposit or any part of it.

8.6. If the Deposit is insufficient the Tenant shall pay to the Landlord such additional sums as required to cover all costs, charges and expenses properly due within a period of 14 days from the end of the tenancy.

8.7. If either party is not contactable or otherwise not responsive at the end of the tenancy, the other party should notify the Deposit scheme administrator so that the Deposit may be treated in accordance with the terms of the scheme.

Obligations of the Tenant

The following clauses set out what is expected of the Tenant during the tenancy in addition to the main terms found in this agreement. If any of these terms are breached, the Landlord may be entitled to deduct monies from the Deposit, claim damages from the Tenant, and/or seek the court's permission to have the Tenant evicted from the Premises because of the breach.

The Tenant agrees:

9.1. That any obligation upon the Tenant under this agreement to do or not to do anything shall also require the Tenant not to permit or cause any licensee or visitor to breach that obligation.

9.2. To pay the Rent as specified earlier in this agreement whether or not it has been formally demanded. The first payment of Rent shall be paid directly to London Realty International. After this the Tenant will be notified in writing of the correct payment details to use and they shall pay all further Rent as directed either to London Realty International, or the Landlord directly.

9.3 To pay interest at 3% above the Bank of England base rate upon any Rent in arrears or other monies due under this agreement for more than 14 days calculated from the date upon which it became due to the date of payment.

9.4. Unless otherwise agreed in writing with the Landlord, to pay for all gas, electricity, water and sewerage services consumed on or supplied to the Premises during the Term, and for all charges made for the use of the telephone (if any), TV licence (if any), TV service (if any), and Internet service (if any) during the Term. This includes standing charges and other similar charges and VAT, as well as charges for actual consumption.

9.5. Unless otherwise agreed in writing with the Landlord, to pay the Council Tax in respect of the Premises for the duration of the Tenancy regardless of legal liability for the Council Tax. If the Council Tax billing authority bills the Landlord for Council Tax for the Premises and other property together, the Tenant agrees to pay a proportionate share of the Council Tax. If the Tenant qualifies for a discount or an exemption from Council Tax it is the responsibility of the Tenant to apply for this.

9.6. That if the Tenant breaches this agreement or fails to fulfil their obligations contained in this agreement, the Tenant shall pay any reasonable costs properly incurred by the Landlord in remedying such breaches or in connection with the enforcement of those obligations.

9.7. To keep the Premises and the Landlord's contents in as good and clean state of repair and condition and decoration as the Premises were in at the commencement of the Term and make good all damage and breakages to the Premises which may occur during the Term (fair wear and tear excepted).

9.8. Not to remove any of the Landlord's contents from the Premises.

9.9. To comply with all statutory requirements upon the Tenant in respect of the Premises and contents. This includes (but is not limited to) not bringing into the Premises any furniture, furnishings or personal items that do not comply with the Furniture and Furnishings (Fire) (Safety) Regulations 1988.

9.10. Not to damage the Premises or the building or make any alteration or addition to it, nor damage or alter the electrical or plumbing system.

9.11. Not to decorate or change the style or colour of the decoration without written consent from the Landlord.

9.12. Not to damage interior walls or decorations by affixing pictures, mirrors, or any other hanging item using nails, screws, adhesive compounds or tapes without written consent from the Landlord.

9.13. Where readily accessible, and with due regard to personal safety, to keep the drains, gutters and pipes of the Premises free from obstruction and clear of any leaves or debris.

9.14. If applicable, to keep the garden, patio, paths, balcony or terrace, (if any), in a neat and tidy condition, swept where necessary and weeded. To maintain any lawns, trees and shrubs. Not to alter the layout of the garden.

9.15. To keep clean the windows inside and outside of the Premises, where safe access is possible. Failure by the Tenant to take adequate precautions to prevent glass panes being cracked or broken will result in the Tenant having to pay for any ensuing damage.

9.16. If there are common parts to the building, not to obstruct, keep or leave anything in them.

9.17. To keep the exterior free from rubbish.

9.18. To place all refuse in plastic bags in the designated dustbin(s) which should be kept in the area provided. If necessary on refuse collection day to move the dustbin(s) to the collection point as required by the local Council.

9.19. Not to hang clothes or other articles on any balcony or out of any window.

9.20. To replace any light bulbs, fluorescent tubes, fuses or batteries promptly and when necessary.

9.21. To notify the Landlord immediately regarding, and confirm in writing as soon as practical thereafter, any defect in the Premises which comes to the Tenant's attention and which is the responsibility of the Landlord to repair. Failure to do so will result in the tenant having to pay the Landlord all liabilities which may be incurred by the Landlord as a result of any such defect not having been so notified.

9.22. To work with the Landlord to minimise the risk caused by Legionella bacteria and in particular to keep showerheads and taps clean, not to interfere with or adjust the boiler temperature, and to run the taps in order to flush through the plumbing system after any prolonged period of inactivity.

9.23. To take reasonable precautions to prevent any damage to the Premises resulting from 'freezing-up'. This includes ensuring the Premises are adequately heated during periods of cold weather to ensure the water system does not freeze. Failure by the Tenant to take such precautions will result in the Tenant having to pay for any ensuing damage.

9.24. To take all reasonable precautions to prevent condensation and damp by keeping the Premises adequately ventilated and heated.

9.25. To use the Premises solely for the purposes of a private residence for the Tenant and any other persons specially permitted by Landlord to occupy the Premises.

9.26. Not to register a business at the Premises, and not to carry on or permit to be carried on at the Premises any trade or business other than a home business as defined by section 43ZA of the Landlord and Tenant Act 1954.

9.27. Not to use the Premises for any immoral, illegal or improper purposes.

9.28. To make only reasonable use of the utilities and communications services consistent with ordinary residential use.

9.29. Not to do or permit to be done in the Premises or elsewhere anything which may be or become a nuisance, annoyance or inconvenience to the Landlord, the owner or occupiers of any adjoining property, the neighbours, other adjoining residents or people in the immediate area.

9.30. Not to keep any cat, dog (excluding guide dogs where reasonably necessary), bird or other pet or animal at the Premises without the Landlord's written consent, such consent, if granted, to be revocable at will by the Landlord upon giving reasonable written notice. If consent is given, the Tenant agrees to undertake, or alternatively pay for, a full clean of the Premises with de-infestation cleaner upon termination of the tenancy.

9.31. Not to fix or suffer to be fixed to the exterior or windows of the Premises any notice board, sign, advertisement poster or aerial without the prior written consent of the Landlord.

9.32. Not to install or change any door locks or alarm codes without the Landlord's prior express written consent (not to be unreasonably withheld), and agree that the Landlord should hold a spare set of keys. In the event of the loss of a key or other security device giving access to the Premises, the Tenant agrees to pay any reasonable costs incurred by the Landlord as a result.

9.33. Not to erect external aerials or satellite dishes without the prior written consent of the Landlord.

9.34. Not to install any gas appliances unless authorised by the Landlord and installed by a registered Gas Safe fitter.

9.35. Not to do anything on the Premises which may invalidate any insurance of the Premises against fire or increase the ordinary premium for such insurance.

9.36. Not to undertake any activity that materially increases the risk of fire or other damage to the Premises or its fixtures and fittings. This includes, without limitation, the storage of dangerous or flammable goods at the Premises, leaving electrical appliances such as tumble dryers on while the Premises are empty, or any other action that unreasonably increases the risk of damage.

9.37. To routinely test the operation of all smoke alarms and replace the batteries when necessary, and to advise the Landlord immediately should any alarm cease to function or be considered non-operational.

9.38. Not to assign sublet or part with or share possession of the Premises or any part of it nor allow the Premises to be occupied by anyone other than the Tenant and no more than the maximum number of permitted persons (the Occupancy), without the prior written consent of the Landlord.

9.39. Not to grant any licensees, take in any lodger, paying guest or person staying on either a permanent or semi-permanent basis without the prior written consent of the Landlord.

9.40. To notify the Landlord if the Tenant is to be absent from the Premises for a period exceeding 14 days. Such notification shall be made at least 5 days prior to the commencement of the period of absence and shall state the actual dates over which the Premises will be unoccupied.

9.41. To take all reasonable steps to protect the Premises from frozen or burst pipes or other damage, if the Premises are left vacant for any period.

9.42. To permit the Landlord, and any superior landlord, or the Landlord's employees/agents at all reasonable times after giving the Tenant at least 24 hours' notice (except in an emergency):

- to enter the Premises to inspect the same and the Landlord's furniture and effects therein (if any) and to carry out any works of maintenance or repair to the Premises or elsewhere which the Landlord may consider necessary. If the Tenant fails to allow access and such failure causes the Landlord to incur costs, the Tenant shall be liable for all reasonable losses resulting as a consequence.
- to enter and view the Premises with any prospective future Tenants or purchasers during the last 60 days of the tenancy.

9.43. At the end of the Term, to vacate the Premises and give vacant possession. The Premises and its content must at the end of the Term be in the same good and clean state of repair and decoration as the Premises was in at the commencement of the Term (fair wear and tear excepted). The tenant must pay for the repair or replacement of any items of the fixtures, fittings and appliances which have been damaged, destroyed or lost.

9.44. At the end of the Term, to remove all of their furniture and other goods from the Premises. The Tenant may be liable for damages if they leave items at the Premises which prevent the Landlord from making use of or re-letting the Premises, or if the Landlord incurs costs in relation to such items (for example, reasonable charges for removal or storage).

9.45. To return all sets of keys of the Premises to the Landlord by 2pm on the day of vacating the Premises, otherwise all reasonable costs of gaining entry to the Premises and resecuring the Premises will be borne by the Tenant.

9.46. To co-operate in the checking of any inventory and/or schedule of condition. The Landlord will bear the costs of preparing the inventory and/or schedule of condition and associated check-in or check-out report. The Tenant agrees to take all reasonable steps to ensure that such a report can be completed, and that they will be liable for any additional costs arising as a result of the Tenant's actions. Those are including but not limited to call-out fees from missed appointments, or any other losses or costs.

9.47. Not to smoke inside the Premises, or permit others to smoke inside the Premises, without the Landlord's written consent. Such consent, if granted, to be revocable at will by the Landlord upon giving reasonable written notice.

9.48. To provide a forwarding address at the end of the tenancy, if requested by the Landlord.

9.49. To forward any notice, order or proposal affecting the Premises or its boundaries to the Landlord within 5 days of receiving it.

Furniture

If the letting includes the use of furniture and effects:

10.1. Where requested by the Landlord, the furniture and effects shall be as specified in an inventory signed by the Tenant.

10.2. The Tenant will:

- Not damage or remove from the Premises any furniture or effects.
- Make good all damage (except fair wear and tear) and breakages to the furniture and effects which may occur during the Term.
- Leave the furniture and effects at the end of the tenancy in the same position as they were at the commencement of the Term.
- Clean or pay for the cleaning of all carpets, curtains and any other parts of the Premises or contents included in the letting which may have been soiled during the tenancy.

Obligations of the Landlord

The following clauses set out what can be expected from the Landlord during the tenancy. If any of these terms are broken, the Tenant may be entitled to claim damages from the Landlord, or ask a court to make the Landlord fulfil their obligations.

The Landlord agrees:

Quiet Enjoyment

11.1. To allow the Tenant to quietly hold and enjoy the Premises during the tenancy without any unlawful interruption by the Landlord or any person rightfully claiming on behalf of the Landlord.

Consents

11.2. To confirm that all necessary consents have been obtained to enable the Landlord to enter this agreement (whether from superior landlords, lenders, mortgagees, insurers, or others).

Statutory Repairing Obligations

11.3. To comply with the obligations to repair the Premises as set out in sections 11 to 16 of the Landlord and Tenant Act 1985 (as amended by the Housing Act 1988). These sections impose on the Landlord obligations to repair and keep in good order:

- the structure of the Premises and exterior (including drains, gutters and pipes);
- certain installations for the supply of water, electricity and gas;
- sanitary appliances including basins, sinks, baths and sanitary conveniences;
- space heating and water heating;

but not other fixtures, fittings, and appliances for making use of the supply of water and electricity. This obligation arises only after notice has been given to the Landlord by the Tenant regarding the defect or issue in question.

11.4. To repay to the Tenant any reasonable costs incurred by the Tenant to remedy the failure of the Landlord to comply with his statutory obligations as stated in clause 11.3 above.

11.5. To comply with the obligation under section 9A of the Landlord and Tenant Act 1985 to keep the Premises fit for human habitation for the duration of the Term.

Insurance

11.6. To insure the building of the Premises under a general household policy with a reputable insurer.

11.7. To provide a copy of the relevant insurance certificate and policy to the Tenant at the start of the tenancy or as soon as possible thereafter.

Other Repairs

11.8. To keep in repair and proper working order all mechanical and electrical items belonging to the Landlord and forming part of the fixtures and fittings, unless the lack of repair is due to the negligence or misuse of the Tenant, his family, or visitors.

11.9. To provide assistance to the Tenants with keeping the Premises free from all pests or vermin as well as remedying any damage caused by pests or vermin.

Safety Regulations

11.10. To ensure that all the furniture and equipment provided by the Landlord complies with the Furniture and Furnishings (Fire) (Safety) Regulations 1988 (as amended in 1993).

11.11. To ensure that all gas appliances comply with the Gas Safety (Installation and Use) Regulations 1998 and that a copy of the safety check record is given to the Tenant at the start of the tenancy.

11.12. To ensure that all electrical installations at the Premises are inspected and tested at regular intervals by a qualified person and that all relevant electrical safety standards (including those under the Electrical Safety Standards in the Private Rented Sector (England) Regulations 2020 where applicable) are met during the tenancy.

Possessions and Refuse

11.13. To remove or pay for the removal of all the possessions of the Landlord (excluding any furnishings, fixtures and fittings that are included with the tenancy) and any rubbish prior to the start of the tenancy.

Interrupting or Ending this Agreement

The following clauses set out the ways in which this agreement may be brought to an end by either party. In addition, these clauses set out the procedures which the Tenant or Landlord shall use when the tenancy is brought to an end.

Early termination by the Landlord

12.1. If and whenever during the Term:

- the Rent or any part of it is in arrears for 14 days after it has become due (whether legally demanded or not), or
- there is a breach of any of the obligations or agreements on the part of the Tenant, or
- the Tenant becomes bankrupt or insolvent or enters into a voluntary arrangement with its creditors; or
- any of the Grounds 2, 7 (in England only), 7A, 7B (in England only), 8, 10-15 and 17 set out in Schedule 2 of the Housing Act 1988 apply

the Landlord may re-enter upon the Premises or any part in the name of the whole resuming possession on the furniture and effects and immediately thereon the tenancy shall terminate, but without prejudice to the other rights and remedies of the Landlord. The Landlord's rights under this clause are subject to the restrictions of the Protection From Eviction Act 1977 and the Housing Act 1988 and the Landlord will not whilst the Tenant is residing in the Premises physically retake possession without first obtaining a Court Order.

Notice to end the tenancy at or after the end of the Initial Term

12.2. If either party wishes to end the tenancy on or after the final day of the Initial Term, they may give notice in writing to the other as follows:

- The Landlord must give notice of no less than two months, such notice to expire any time on or after the final day of the Initial Term. A notice served by the Landlord under section 21 of the Housing Act 1988 shall be sufficient notice under this clause.
- The Tenant must give notice of no less than one month, such notice to expire the day before a Rent Payment Day or on the final day of the Initial Term.

12.3. If neither party serves a valid notice to terminate the tenancy at the end of the Initial Term, the parties agree that at the end of the Initial Term the tenancy will continue as a contractual periodic tenancy on a monthly basis.

Uninhabitability

12.4. If at any time the Premises are rendered uninhabitable by an event or events which are not the result of negligence or breach of contract by either party then, the choice being at the Landlord's sole discretion, either:

- the Rent will cease to be payable by the Tenant until the Premises are made habitable and the Landlord will be under no obligation to provide alternative accommodation; or
- the Rent will continue to be payable and the Landlord will be obligated to provide suitable alternative accommodation to the Tenant.

12.5. If following an event described above, in the reasonable opinion of an appropriate expert the Premises cannot be made habitable within one month then either party may give one month's notice to terminate this agreement following which it will end and no further obligations under it will be performable by either party save that either party may pursue the other for breaches of this agreement which pre-date said termination.

Mutual Break Clause

12.6. The Initial Term of this tenancy agreement may be terminated by either party giving the other at least two months' notice in writing, such notice not to expire until at least 6 months after the start of the Term. A notice served by the Landlord under section 21 of the Housing Act 1988 shall be sufficient notice under this clause.

The Tenant is obliged to pay rent up to and including the termination date, so if the tenancy is terminated on a date which is not the last day of a rental period, the rent due for any incomplete rental periods will be apportioned accordingly.

Effect of Notices to terminate the tenancy

12.7. On the expiry of a notice to terminate the tenancy under clause 12.2 or 12.6 the tenancy shall end and no further obligations shall be performed under the tenancy save that either party may pursue the other for any breach of this agreement occurring before the expiry of the notice.

Notices & Miscellaneous

Notices

13.1. The Landlord gives notice to the Tenant that pursuant to Section 48(1) of the Landlord and Tenant Act 1987 that notices (including notices in proceedings) may be served on the Landlord at the address specified at the beginning of this agreement.

13.2. Any notice served upon the Tenant by the Landlord pursuant to this agreement or any statute or regulation must be served in writing and will be deemed sufficiently served if sent by registered post or first class post to or left at the Premises. Notices served by recorded delivery post, or prepaid first class post to the Premises, shall be deemed to have been properly served and received by the Tenant on the second day after posting (or if that day is not a working day on the next working day), or in the case of notices left at the Premises on the next working day after delivery.

13.3. The Landlord and the Tenant agree that notices pursuant to this agreement may be served on the other party by email. The email addresses for notice are:

Landlord: (Notice email visible once signed)

Tenant: (Notice email visible once all tenants have signed)

13.4. Notice served by email shall be deemed sufficiently served if it is sent to the Tenant or the Landlord at the email addresses identified above in this agreement and no notification of failure to deliver that email is received. Notices served by email will be deemed served on the next working day after sending.

13.5. The Landlord gives the Tenant notice under the Housing Act 1988 that possession may be recovered on the following grounds:

- The Landlord notified the Tenant that the Landlord previously occupied the Premises as the Landlord's only or principal home and the Landlord may rely on Ground 1 of Schedule 2 to the Housing Act 1988 to recover possession of the Premises in circumstances where the Landlord requires the Premises as the Landlord's only or principal home.
- The Landlord notified the Tenant that the Premises are subject to a mortgage granted prior to the start of the tenancy for purposes of Ground 2 of Schedule 2 to the Housing Act 1988 and has served notice in accordance with Ground 1 of Schedule 2 to the Housing Act 1988.

Miscellaneous

14.1. If the Premises comprise part only of a building the letting shall include the use (in common with others) of access ways to and from the Premises inside the building.

14.2. Where two or more persons are named on the tenancy agreement, their obligations shall be joint and several. This means, for example, that any one or more of the individuals jointly forming the Tenant can at the Landlord's sole discretion be held responsible for the full Rent and other obligations under the agreement if the other individuals do not fulfil their obligations.

14.3. References to masculine gender include the feminine; to the singular include the plural; and to the 'month' mean calendar month.

14.4. References to a working day mean a week day excluding Christmas Day, Good Friday and any day which, under the Banking and Financial Dealings Act 1971, is a bank holiday in England and Wales.

14.5. The Tenant is responsible for insuring their own belongings, furniture and furnishings in the Premises, and the Landlord will not accept liability for any loss or damage that may occur as a result of use within the Premises.

14.6. The Landlord and the Tenant confirm their agreement with the **London Realty International** Terms & Conditions and Privacy Policy which they made when creating their account.

14.7. Where the Landlord's own title to the Premises is leasehold and not freehold, the Landlord may themselves be a tenant under a superior lease. The Tenant agrees to perform and observe at all times during the Term the conditions and stipulations contained in the superior lease that were notified to the Tenant prior to the commencement of the tenancy.

14.8. The Landlord is responsible for ensuring the Premises comply with any applicable property licensing regulations for the duration of the tenancy. The Tenant agrees not to use the Premises in any manner which might lead to it becoming licensable under any part of the Housing Act 2004 without the Landlord's express written consent.

14.9. If any term of this agreement is, in whole or in part, held to be illegal or unenforceable to any extent under any enactment or rule of law, that term or part shall to that extent be deemed not to form part of this agreement and the enforceability of the remainder of this agreement shall not be affected.

14.10. The Landlord and the Tenant agree that this agreement shall be exclusively governed by and interpreted in accordance with the laws of England and Wales.

14.11. The operation of section 62 of the Law of Property Act 1925 is excluded from this agreement. The only rights granted to the Tenant are those expressly set out in this agreement, and the Tenant is not to be entitled to any other rights affecting any adjoining property of the Landlord.

The Guarantor

The Guarantor is the person or persons responsible for discharging the Tenant's obligations if the Tenant defaults whether the Landlord elects to pursue the Tenant or not.

"Joint and Several" means that the Guarantor will be liable with the Tenant to pay all Rent and any debt arising from any breach of the tenancy until all debt is paid in full.

15.1. In consideration of the Landlord agreeing at the request of the Guarantor to accept the Tenant as the Tenant of the Premises the Guarantor hereby covenants with the Landlord that the Tenant will pay the Rent and comply with all the Tenant's obligations in this Agreement (including any variations to increase the Rent whether by agreement between the Landlord and the Tenant or pursuant to a notice given by the Landlord under section 13 of the Housing Act 1988). In any case of default by the Tenant, the Guarantor will pay the Landlord damages in respect of the Landlord's reasonable losses incurred as a result of that default.

15.2. As between the Landlord and the Guarantor the Guarantor is a principal debtor and not merely a surety.

15.3. This Guarantee is irrevocable and shall continue beyond the Guarantor's death or bankruptcy (falling as a liability on the estate) throughout the period that the Premises are occupied by the Tenant and is not limited to the Term of this agreement.

15.4. If the Tenant defaults during the initial Term or any extension, renewal or continuation of this agreement or the Tenant is declared bankrupt and the Tenant's Trustee in Bankruptcy elects to disclaim the agreement then on written demand the Guarantor hereby agrees to pay damages to the Landlord for all losses, claims, liabilities, costs and expenses arising out of or in connection with that default or disclaimer or incurred by the Landlord in connection with the default or disclaimer.

15.5. It is hereby agreed that the Guarantor's liability under this Clause will be joint and several with the Tenant which means that each will be responsible for complying with the Tenant's obligations under this agreement both individually and together. The Landlord may seek to enforce these obligations and claim damages against the Tenant, the Guarantor, or both of them under these clauses. These obligations will not be cleared or affected by any act, neglect, leniency, or giving of time by the Landlord endeavouring to obtain payment or in the enforcement of the Tenant's covenants. If the Tenant surrenders any part of the Premises the Guarantor's liability will continue in respect of the part not surrendered. Any liability accumulated at the date of surrender will continue unaffected.

15.6. If requested by the Landlord, the Guarantor agrees to provide written confirmation of their current address at the start of the tenancy and to notify the Landlord in writing if they move to a new address in the course of the tenancy.

Custom Clause Notice

The clauses defined under Custom Clauses below, have been written by the Landlord in agreement with the Tenant. The clauses have not been vetted by London Realty International are not endorsed by London Realty International, and have been added against the explicit recommendation of London Realty International. London Realty International can not offer advice on the contents of this section and recommends independent legal advice is sought before agreeing to any clauses outlined in this section.

Note that individual terms and conditions in earlier sections of this agreement may be replaced or modified by the Custom Clauses set out below, with the exception of clause 3 and clause 4 which are essential to the Rent Now process and cannot be modified or replaced.

Custom Clauses

Custom Clause 1. This is an example of a custom clause. If no custom clauses are specified, this page will be omitted from the contract.

Contract Digitally Signed By

Here is a list of people set out to sign the contract, and signatures where they have been collected.

Where signatures have been collected dates and times are displayed in Coordinated Universal Time (UTC).

The Tenant

Signature	Printed Name	Date Signed	Email (verified)	IP Address
- _____	Tenant		Visible once signed	

The Guarantor

Signature	Printed Name	Date Signed	Email (verified)	IP Address
- _____	Guarantor		Visible once signed	

The Landlord

Signature	Printed Name	Date Signed	Email (verified)	IP Address
- _____	Landlord		Visible once signed	

www.ingramcontent.com/pod-product-compliance
Lightning Source LLC
Chambersburg PA
CBHW060437220526
45465CB00008B/3175